Lily's Scrap-book

LILY'S SCRAP-BOOK.

LILY'S SCRAP-BOOK.

LILY'S SCRAP-BOOK

BY

MRS. SALE BARKER

AUTHOR OF "LITTLE WIDEAWAKE."

WITH ONE HUNDRED AND TWENTY PICTURES

LONDON AND NEW YORK
GEORGE ROUTLEDGE AND SONS
1877

CONTENTS.

Contents.

Contents.

Contents.

LILY'S SCRAP-BOOK.

Now, then, Lily darling, let us begin to paste the pictures into your Scrap-Book; we have plenty left from the Nursery Screen. What shall we begin with? Look here! let us take this pretty picture of a dear little girl. She is something like my

B.

Lily, I declare. She has been gathering wild flowers, you see, and is carrying them home in her little apron.

Now, dear children, you must all help. Make haste and find more pictures; there are plenty in the drawer. What does Lily hand me next? Oh!

this is a poor gipsy woman carrying her tiny baby on her back. She is just like that one who came to the garden gate the other day, and wanted to tell us all our fortunes. I daresay she has wandered many a weary mile with her precious little bundle on her back. Her husband and some more chil-dren are there, sitting round the fire, watching the boiling of the pot. And, I declare, I see a nice old donkey, too, in the distance.

This is a magpie, who has been hung up in his cage, outside some house; and you see a hawk

has come to peck at the poor prisoner, or perhaps has been stealing his food. The magpie has caught him by the claw, and seems to hold him tight too. I think it serves him right.

Look at this fireman in the flame and smoke!
That is his son holding up the hose for him, and
learning to be brave like his father.

Yes, Johnny dear, this is, as you say, a very
curious looking bird. It is called a Grebe. What
odd little black tufts it has sticking up on its head,
and how strange that black ring looks round its
neck! Its breast is silvery white, with a little tint

of cinnamon colour here and there; and this part of
the bird is often used for trimming ladies' mantles,
in the place of fur. You see by its feet that it is
a species of duck; and it builds its nest among
reeds in shallow water, twisting the reeds into the
nest to support it

Now, Johnny, see if you can find something funny to come next : we've not had anything to make us laugh yet. Yes, these two pictures are funny, certainly. There is the same man and boy in each. Paste them next to each other in the book. And I suppose I must try to make up a little story for them. I think that gentleman

dressed in a plaid suit looks like an English tourist ; and, judging by the wooden shoes of the boy, I should say the scene must be in France. The gentleman has had that suit of clothes made on purpose to wear during his summer holiday abroad ; and the hat matches the clothes, which is a very neat idea. By way of practising his French, he is talking to that little peasant boy, who has the care of the ducks and geese for some farmer. The man and boy are sitting side by side, and

staring as if each thought the other rather a
ridiculous figure. There is a stream close by, and
the boy shows the English gentleman a little
wooden bridge, close to a mill. When he is on
the bridge, the Englishman stops, and leans upon
the railing, while he watches some ducks in the
water. The railing gives way, and down he comes,

souse, into the water himself, frightening the ducks
nearly to death, besides causing great alarm to a
man who is standing by, and to the little boy who
is watching him from the bank of the stream.
Indeed, the boy is so astonished and alarmed that
he jumps up, as you see, right out of his wooden
shoes. The water is shallow, and the Englishman
is not drowned. He soon scrambles out, and the
good people of the mill let him warm himself at
their fire; but we may suppose he caught a bad cold.

How attentive these two little girls are to their
music lesson! And I can see that they play well,

too. I am as sure of it as if I could hear them.
That must be either their mamma or the gover-
ness who stands behind them, and she seems well
satisfied with her pupils.

Dear little boy! how nicely he has gone to sleep with his new toy-horse cuddled up to him so close. Now, I wonder whom that little boy reminds me of! Can you guess, Johnny? I think I know some one who is very fond of taking his toys into

bed with him, even when they are hard, and have awkward corners, like the horse in the picture! I fancy such toys may be uncomfortable bedfellows, if you happen to roll over them in the night; but, no doubt, it is a pleasure, on opening your eyes the first thing in the morning, to find the pretty new toy there, close to you, that you have just been dreaming about.

Dear me! this is dreadful. A tiny duckling
gobbled up by that great ostrich! And see! the

mother duck, in her despair, attacks the monster.
But let us turn to something more cheerful.

Look! this is another picture of ostriches; but here they are in their natural wi d state, and in their native country, where there are no poor little ducklings for them to gobble up. I like them better here. Those pyramids you see in the distance show that the country in the picture is in-

tended for Egypt. In that part of the world are great plains of sand where the ostriches run about; for you must know that their wings are too small to raise them from the ground; but, to make amends, they can run as fast as a horse with their long legs. You may see some ostriches at the Zoological Gardens.

Here we have a fiddler playing away merrily. He is sitting on a table with his jug and glass beside him, and enters so thoroughly into the spirit of his music, that you see his own feet are dancing a jig while his hands hold the fiddle and bow. These fiddlers used to be thought a great deal of in country villages, years ago. They were

welcome everywhere; and were present at all the harvest-homes, and weddings, and out-of-door dances, and merry-makings, that, in the good old times, were held in country places. Things have much changed in England of late years, but in Ireland the strolling fiddler is still in great request. He carries about the latest gossip from place to place, and is often as famous for his fun and wit as for his fiddling.

The summer merry-makings in country villages at the present day, do not often amount to any-thing more important than a feast given to the children of the village school; and that is just what is represented in this picture. The children

have had a treat of tea and plum-cake, and now are having games upon the village green. The game they are playing is called "Kiss-in-the-Ring." They form a ring by taking hold of hands, while two of them run in and out, one trying to catch the other, under the uplifted arms, the pur-suer following in the exact footsteps of the other.

This young man has been away from home,
seeking his fortune in the world.   He is now re-

turning to his native village, which he just catches
the first glimpse of, down in the valley, as he comes
across the mountains.   How his face lightens up,
while he waves his hat with joy !

Here is a picture which will just fit in to fill up this page. A good little boy has come to feed his pet raven. Mr. Raven has been let out of his cage, and has perched himself just opposite his little master, with his beak wide open, ready for his

breakfast. Does he not look eager and greedy for his food? I can fancy him croaking in an angry voice. The little boy holds up his finger to the raven, and is giving him a lecture upon good manners at his meals; saying: "Now just have a little patience, and don't appear so greedy."

Yes, Cissy, my darling, I tnink this pretty picture of two dear little calves will do nicely here. They are very like our own two pretty little Alderney calves out in the field there, Ruby and Diamond. Dear little gentle things ! You would hardly suppose that they will one day grow into such sedate, serious-looking creatures as their mothers are. Do

you know, dears, when I was a little girl, I once had a pet calf, that knew me quite well, and followed me about, and liked being stroked and patted, just as a dog or a horse does. Primrose was the name I gave her, I remember, because the first day I saw the little creature I also found the first primrose of the year.

Here is the picture which must come next : you see it is a picture of a yoke of oxen. Fancy the two happy, careless little calves, we have just been looking at, ever turning into these hard-working, steady oxen, with that great yoke upon their necks, and those rings in their noses. In England we do not use oxen much in this way now, though they may still be seen in some parts drawing the plough ; but, in many countries on the Continent,

they are not only used in farm labour, but for drawing carts, when much speed is not required. In India. bullocks are used very generally, and particularly for drawing a kind of carriage in which you can lie down, called a gharry or bandy. But the bullocks of India are rather different from those of. Europe : they have a hump between the shoulders, and, besides, they are much more active.

C

Ha! ha! ha! This hunter has hit upon an original plan for attracting those antelopes. A man

the wrong end upwards, no longer looks like one; and those silly creatures are evidently curious to know what it is they see. Once within gunshot, they will find out the truth to their cost.

Johnny brings me a picture of a great lion. I sincerely hope he is not roaming about anywhere near our friend in the last picture, who has turned himself upside down in order to have a shot at the poor antelopes. If the lion once caught sight of the gentleman, no matter which end might be uppermost, it would be the worse for him. The hunter would be hunted pretty soon. You remember the

lions, my children, in the Zoological Gardens, do you not ? Well, you saw what strong, grand, noble creatures they are ; but also how terrible ! I should not like to live in a country where you could ever meet a lion face to face ; yet this may happen in many parts of Africa. Fancy a poor settler in some of our African colonies hearing a lion roaring outside at night, and knowing that the creature is prowling about, seeking what he may devour.

Now, this is a sad picture. It shows us a little boy having a bad tumble. You see he has been running much too fast down that steep hill. His name is Johnny Fleetfoot, but his feet did not get on as fast as his body this time, for it has left them

quite behind. Indeed, his nose seems to have been anxious to get on before anything else, and has suffered in consequence: he has come down right upon it, I fear. Luckily he has a kind brother and sister, who were out with him, and they are helping him up. Boys soon get over such accidents, and so, I hope, will Johnny Fleetfoot.

Well, here's something very curious. Can this be the old woman in the nursery song who sang, "Dilly, dilly, duckling, come and be killed?" She

looks as if she had come down to the pond to catch a duck for her dinner, and the duck, instead, is thinking about having some dinner himself. The duck certainly seems to be having the best of it as yet.

The engine-drivers on our railways are rough
and weather-beaten figures, like that in the picture.
The life is a hard one : on, on they go at the rate
of forty or fifty miles an hour in all weather,
through cutting wind, or rain, or driving snow.
But whatever his appearance, the engine-driver is
a fine fellow.   He has—that is, at least, if he is fit

for his post—some great qualities. His own safety,
and that of all who travel in the train, depend
upon his care, his watchfulness, and presence of
mind.   It is for him to slacken speed, or hasten
on, as he thinks best : it is for him to watch the
signals as the train advances, to read the signs of
safety or of danger.   And we may imagine how
anxious he must sometimes be when he can see
nothing on account of fog or driving snow.

Oh, what have we here, Lily dear ? A beautiful
fairy, I declare; or, at least, a beautiful girl dressed

up as one. I think she is acting in a drawing-
room, and coming from behind a curtain to dance.
It is a charming little picture.

This shows us the father of the family just come
home from his day's work, or perhaps from a long

journey. The mother remains in the hut cooking
the supper, while all the children rush out, so glad
to see papa again. And not less glad than the
children is the good old doggie.

Here is another nice doggie, making himself useful, and showing his affection for his master and
mistress by taking care of the baby. Mamma is
working somewhere in the field. She cannot leave
baby at home, because she has no one to take

care of him : so while she works, she puts baby
to sleep under a tree, and bids Tip guard him.
There sits Tippy, the curly-tailed doggie, so
quiet that the little birds in their nest above
are not at all frightened, but chirp away quite
happily.

This picture reminds us that doggies are not all nice. It represents the old fable of the dog in the manger. A dog once jumped into a manger which had been filled with hay for some oxen, and he barked at them whenever they came near him

to eat. He could not eat the hay himself, yet he prevented those from enjoying it who could have done so. Was he not spiteful and bad? People are often compared to the dog in the manger when they are selfish and unkind as he was.

This is a picture of an old hermit in his cell. You see he is reading his Bible, and has a skull beside him. There, too, is his rosary, with a cruci- fix attached, hanging near; and he has an hour- glass also close at hand to remind him continually how short this life is in comparison with eternity. These her.nits were men who retired from the

world, and shut themselves up in some hut or cave. There, living in solitude, they spent their days in praying, and fasting, and sometimes in scourging themselves, all under the idea that by such suffer- ing here they would merit heaven hereafter. There are no hermits nowadays, even in Roman Catholic countries, which is lucky, in my opinion ; for, while the poor men made their own lives miserable, they certainly did not promote the happiness of any- body.

Here, Lily, you have brought me a picture of a mule and muleteer. You see how carefully they are picking their way down that hill: the poor mule is heavily laden, and can scarcely steady himself. In Spain, and some other mountainous countries, mules are more used than horses or donkeys. The fact is, they are more sure-footed

than either. Among the Pyrenees, and in other mountainous parts of Spain, where many of the roads are unfit for any kind of carriage, mules convey merchandise and packages of all kinds upon their backs Sometimes a whole string of them may be seen, one after another, carrying merchandise across the mountain passes. The muleteer in the picture is a Spaniard, as we may see by his dress, and by the cigarette he is smoking.

But even mules, sure-footed as they are, cannot always be relied upon, as you see, my children, in

this terrible picture. Here it appears, though, as if part of the rock itself had given way, and mule-leader and mule-rider are both falling down the cruel mountain side.

Why, what a merry party this is, out in the snow! These children are May, and Etta, and Tommy. May, you see, is pushing little Etta.

along in a sort of sledge. Etta has mamma's muff; she is wrapped up warm and cosy, and is enjoying the fresh cold air. These three children all like the cold weather, and think nothing would be nicer than to live far away up somewhere in the north. But they do not know what real cold weather is, and would not like it so much if they always had it, I can tell them. Here Cissy has just found me a picture of a Laplander, who lives in a country where it is terribly cold, and where, during nearly half the year, they never see the sun. You ask if

the Laplanders are happy. Well, I daresay they are happy in their way; but I should think their ideas of happiness do not extend to much beyond keeping themselves warm, and getting enough to eat. Still, our friend in the picture looks very comfortable, wrapped up in his warm coat of fur, and with that cap drawn down over his ears, sliding along on his snow-shoes.

Why, Johnny brings me another wintry-looking picture; and the scene must I think be laid in Lapland too, for here we have a little girl riding on a reindeer. In Lapland, I must tell you, they use reindeer to draw their sledges about, just as

we use horses to draw our carriages. This kind of deer is as strong, and almost as big, as a horse; but I never heard or read of one being used to ride upon, even by a man, much more a little girl. I fancy the picture must be meant to illustrate a story, not to show anything that really happened.

This monkey was fond of jumping on to horses' backs, so one day his master dressed him up, and strapping him on to an old hunter, sent him after

the hounds. Poor monkey! Away he went, and people wondered who the tiny gentleman could be that rode so fast.

D

Little merry Mabel is going in to say "Good
morning" to dear mamma, who has a headache,

and is breakfasting in bed.   Mabel carries her doll
with her, and intends dolly to have a kiss from
mamma too, after she has had one herself.

This is a picture of the Fox who had lost his tail. According to the fable, his tail had been cut off in a trap; and finding himself conspicuous and rather ridiculous without one, he assembled a good many foxes together, and made them an

eloquent speech. He described the immense advantage and comfort he derived from being without a great heavy bush to drag about behind him; and advised them to cut off all their tails. But a cunning old fox replied, " You only give us this advice because you have lost your own."

Nurse is washing baby-boy, and he doesn't seem quite to like it. He has half a mind to cry, but nurse keeps chattering away all the time, and contrives to amuse him. As she dabs his face with the sponge, she says: " Tell me, Mr. Sponge, is the

little rosy cheek quite clean ? " Then she pretends the sponge is speaking, and says in another voice " Yes, nurse, the cheeks are clean now, but the pretty ears want me to wash them a little more.'; Upon which she sets to work at the ears, and so on. When it comes to the drying, she holds a conversation with the towels, which at last declare :

" Now we've done our work well ; baby-boy is nice and dry, and ready to have his pretty clothes put on." Then on goes, first of all, the little flannel jersey, and that makes a few remarks. If it does not seem to come on easily, it expresses an opinion that baby-boy has grown fatter during the night.

The little socks and the shoes have a word to say also, and as for the dress it makes quite a long speech. Comb and brush smooth out the tangled curls, and say how pretty they are all the time. At last the dressing is all got through, and there has been no crying at all. Do you remember the time, Johnny, not very long ago, when nurse used to manage you in that way while you were dressed ?

. .Here we have a Sparrow-hawk ; not an uncom-
mon bird in England.   It may often be seen high
in the air, remaining poised for several minutes in

one spot : then it suddenly darts down to seize some bird or little field-mouse.

This is a very pretty picture. It is early summer and here we have a farmer's family watching the

swallows coming back, after their long winter's absence, to the nest they built last year. Mamma and the children are all equally glad, I think, to see the pretty birds again ; they welcome them like old friends, and would not hurt or disturb them for the world.

See how fond this soldier is of his little girl!
Perhaps he is going away, and is wishing her good-
bye. He may even be going to fight, and may be
thinking, as he tosses her up in the air, that perhaps it is the last time he will ever see her dear

little face, or hear her sweet merry laugh. She
has no thought of the future, at all events : even
if papa tells her that he may be away a long
time, she hardly understands the difference between that and his coming back to-morrow
Happy childhood !

This picture represents the Duck family: Mr.
and Mrs. Duck, two daughters and two sons; a
charming family, and well to do in the world, I
assure you. See how upright they hold themselves, and how elegantly they are dressed! Though

M.U.SEARS.SC

you and I may not think a duck face pretty, they
are perfectly satisfied with their own looks. The
children playing about on the village green feel
quite abashed at the thought of their raggedness,
and their own merriment, as they watch the Duck
family pompously and solemnly walking past.

- Here is a picture which shows what dangers
hunters meet with, who go out in great forests,

shooting wild animals. They have just shot a
deer, and when the boy, who serves as guide, runs
up to see if it is dead, he is attacked by a wolf.
I hope the hunters are in time to save his life,

This is another picture of hunting wild beasts. The scene must be, I think, in some mountainous

part of Italy or Spain, where wild boars are still to be found. They are strong and very savage beasts. If that hunter misses, or only wounds the boar, it will attack him furiously.

This is little Peter Perkins come out to feed the chickens. They are his particular charge, and every morning—tiny boy as he is—he remembers to trot off to cooky to get the grain for the fowls before he has his own breakfast. Then how the chickens know his little footsteps! and how they come with

hops, skips, jumps, and flutters, to his feet! They are not a bit afraid of him, as you can see in the picture. The little bantam cock Redcap, is indeed too fearless sometimes ; for, as the little boy holds the grain in his hand, master Redcap bobs his head forward, and actually pecks the grain out of the little hand, now and then taking a bit of the soft pink flesh besides.

"Grandmamma dear, how are clocks made?"
says the little boy in the picture.   Grandmamma
opens the clock, and shows the pendulum wagging

from side to side.   Then she tries to explain all
about it, but finds it difficult ; and ends by telling
him he is too little and too young to understand
it yet.

Ah, Johnny dear, so you bring me a picture of
a man in armour. I daresay you know—for you
have seen the armour in the tower—that in old
times men covered themselves up in steel to go to

battle. As soon as fire-arms were used, the armour
had to be made so thick to resist bullets, that men
could no longer bear the weight of an entire suit,
and wore only so much as you see in the picture.
He is a soldier of about the time of Queen Eliza-
beth, and carries an arquebus—the earliest kind of
musket.

This is a soldier too, though a very different sort of figure. You see the coats of mail have been cast aside altogether now; this gentleman wears merely a fine coat, coloured red, a long waistcoat,

breeches and stockings, and a belt to which is attached a sword. His hair is curled and powdered, and instead of a helmet, like our friend that we have just pasted into the book, he has a jaunty three-cornered cocked hat, set rather on one side. This is a soldier of the time of George the Second.

This looks like a fine breezy hill with the wind-mill on it, and I should say a famous place for flying kites. The picture is by a German artist,

and I daresay kites in Germany are made like these, for they are not quite like English kites. I suppose that is a German cap too that the boy on the left-hand side has on.

Poor old man! he is holding up one of his toy lambs to that little girl, and hopes she will ask her mamma to buy it. They are a very simple poor sort of toy, made by himself; only cut out of fire-wood, with some wool gummed over them. He makes

them in his miserable London lodging; then wanders out into the suburbs, where little villas with gardens are dotted about, and persuades the children to buy. Thus he earns a few pennies; while he likes to see the children's faces, and breathe the fresh air.

E

I think my young friend in the picture will hesi-
tate another time before he meddles with carpenters' tools.   This is Tommy Touchall.   He is the
plague of his relations ; always doing mischief, and
meddling with everything.   Sometimes he amuses

himself by turning his mother's work-basket upside
down, and spoiling or losing the contents ; sometimes he scatters his father's papers in the same
way.   One day some carpenters were in the house,
when he got hold of their tools, and cut his hand,
as you see.

This, as you may suppose, is Tommy Touchall again. You would think the pain he felt when he cut his fingers would have cured him of touching things he did not know how to use. But he soon forgot the lesson, and here he is, as you see in the

picture, blowing out the gas without turning it off. The consequence was that the room became filled with gas, and some one going in with a light, there was a terrible explosion, which did a great deal of damage, though by good luck no one was seriously hurt.

You may well laugh, children: this *is* a queer fellow. It is a baboon, called a Gelada; a native

of Africa. Is he not frightful and ridiculous? and yet how sad-looking!

Well, Johnny, you have really found a still uglier monkey. See how he shows his teeth. It is a fero-

cious baboon, called a Mandrill, and is remarkable for a blue patch on each cheek, and a red muzzle.

. Lily has managed to find a picture which shows
us two little people very like herself and my
Johnny. You see these little people are inclined
to meddle with things that they have no business

to touch. There comes the nurse, and just look at
her face! isn't she angry? I must say, my own
opinion is that such little children should not have
been left alone in the room at all, for fear they
should hurt themselves, as well as do mischief.

This is certainly a funny picture, and as puzzling as it is droll. Of all the queer figures, queer faces, and queer hats I ever saw, these

are about the most curious. The fishing-rods in the men's hands do not help us to understand them. I think, my darlings, you must fancy any meaning you can for the picture: I can make nothing of it.

Dear me, dear me! here's poor little Paul Pickle
having a good scolding from his grandpapa!
What do you think he has been about? Why, I
am sorry to say, he put a tiny frog into grandpapa's

inkstand. When grandpapa went to his writing-
table, and settled himself, with all his papers before
him, to go on with his learned treatise on the
human mind, he had no sooner lifted the lid off
the ink than out jumped the little frog. It was
sopping with ink, and leapt first on to the midst of

the papers ; then into grandpapa's lap. Now grandpapa is a learned professor, and has a favourite theory that no well-regulated mind ever feels surprise. Nevertheless, he was surprised and startled. Recovering himself, he suspects the

culprit, whom he finds in the next room, and gives him a good scolding. Returning to his seat, he is trying to persuade himself that he had not been surprised at all, when he is startled by a terrible noise just outside his door, and jumps up from his chair. It is Master Paul, occupied as we see him in the picture. Grandpapa comes out this time with uplifted cane instead of finger.

This is one of the fine Mount St. Bernard dogs, which are kept at a monastery among the Alps.

They go out during snow-storms to look for travellers that may be lost. He has found a boy in the snow, and is carrying him to the monastery.

This is a picture, my darlings, of a poor hard-working creature; yet this woman has something to make her happy. Her fingers move quicker and

quicker to make her pretty lace at the thought that she is earning food for her little child. He is all the world to her; her greatest care and greatest blessing.

This little boy, who in after life became a great
musician, was very poor when young ; so to earn

money, he sometimes played his violin in the
gardens of the Tuileries at Paris, where a crowd
would collect to hear him.

Here is a curious company of friends holding a conversation : a donkey, a hare, a snail, and a swallow. The donkey says : " Mine is a harder life than any of yours ; I get hard blows, and have to work and toil." The hare rejoins : " I would

change with you to-morrow ; I often have to run for my life, though I do no harm to anyone." Says the snail : " Life would be jolly enough, if you were only safe from being trodden upon." And the swallow chirps out : " Make the best of everything, and enjoy summer while it lasts."

This is a picture, dear children, of a poor little girl, whose baby-brother is taken ill with croup in

the night. She has no father, and mother cannot leave baby; so little Mary runs off through the dark night and snow for the doctor, and she soon brings him back with her.

Now, Lily, darling, I certainly think this will be one of the best and funniest pictures in your scrap-book. I have not laughed so much at any as I have at this one. Poor old woman! she must have had enough to do, I'm sure. Look at the poor little creatures fighting and

scrambling about in the shoe. Large as it is, it does not look as if it would hold them all. I am quite sure the old woman's arm must ache with all the whipping it has to give. Now, children, I have quite made up my mind that if ever I go to another fancy ball, I will go as the "Old Woman who lived in a Shoe." And you may be sure I shall carry a birch.

Here is a picture of a labouring man taking
a walk on Sunday accompanied by all his chil-

dren. His is a humble simple life, not free from
cares; and yet a happy one, for there is love
in it.

Here is another picture of a poor cottager, who
finds happiness in loving his children and being
loved by them. He has just returned from his

work, and see how glad they are! Father jumps
baby up in his arms, and the little girl asks for
a kiss, while the boy carries off his father's
spade.

You have read Æsop's fables, Cissy dear, and I daresay you remember the " Ass in the Lion's skin." This must be a picture of that silly donkey ; and I will tell Lily and Johnny what the fable is. There was an ass once who was very vain and ambitious : he got the skin of a lion, and putting

it on himself, was delighted to find how he frightened all the animals he met with in the forest. At last seeing a fox, he tried to frighten him also ; and thinking to make himself yet more terrible, began to bray. The fox, who had turned to run, stopped directly, and said : " You stupid donkey ! if you want to pass for a lion, you should not bray."

Oh! what a miserably bitter night it is; with
snow falling fast! That young man is a shepherd:
He has just brought in his sheep for the night

and lighted his fire, when a poor old man
makes his way to the door, half dead with
cold. The shepherd brings him to the fire,
gives him food and a night's lodging. In the
morning the old man goes upon his way blessing
his kind host.

These children have come to spend the day with
grandmamma at her pretty cottage in the country.
Such visits are a treat for them and her. The

children are pleased because she takes pains to
amuse them, while she delights to hear their laugh-
ter, and to see their bright young faces.

Grandmamma always has some new toys ready for the children, and she is so good-natured that she lets them take her clothes out of her drawers to dress up in. Look how the baby is dressed up in the picture : he means himself to be a king, or perhaps a beadle, or a general, or somebody very grand. Upon his head he has a hood

lined with fur, which grandmamma puts over her own head in winter, if she goes out in the evening. Then he has a large spoon stuck in his belt for a sword, and grandmamma's stick in his hand for a sceptre. The other children are all bowing to him, you see. I think he must be meant for a King, or a Prince of Wales, at least.

What a funny long-legged bird you have brought me, Lily darling! Does it not look like a bird walking upon stilts? Indeed, it is sometimes called ihe Stilt, but the proper name of it is the Long-legged Plover. It is a very handsome bird,

being beautifully marked with white and glossy black. Although more rare than the common plover, it is met with in the same places—in marshes and on the banks of rivers. As you may imagine from the length of its legs, it can run at a famous pace.

Here we have another picture of a bird. The
Great Bustard is not often met with now, though it
used to be common. It is the largest of British
birds. The plumage is brown and black, but the

peculiarity of the bird consists in its having a
pouch in the forepart of the neck, which will con-
tain several pints of water. The nest is always
built on dry sandy downs, where water is scarce
hence the use of the pouch.

It is summer, and the weather is very hot, so these good little girls have gone out into the garden to sit there and learn their lessons. They have placed themselves, as they think, in a nice quiet corner, against the paling in the shade of the trees,

and they little fancy that their brother Tom—that riotous boy, who is home for the holidays—is looking over the paling, watching them. He thinks how lucky he is that he has no lessons to do this hot weather, and he does not leave his sisters long in peace, I can tell you.

This is a picture of a little boy and girl playing up in mamma's bedroom. The little girl has put on mamma's bonnet hind part before, she has papa's bootjack on one arm for a baby, and a basket on

the other. She is pretending to be a poor woman just going out to market. The boy is playing at being a coachman : papa's boots are the horses, and they seem to want a deal of whipping, for he is laying on unmercifully with papa's riding whip.

Here we have a village school. See how the old
schoolmaster stoops over his desk, with spectacles
on his nose, and skull-cap on his head. Some o
the boys are very sharp at their lessons, while some
weary the poor old man by their stupidity till, as
he said one day, they almost made him stupid in
trying to teach them. The genius of the school,

however, is a boy who has a talent for drawing
He always carries about a piece of charcoal in his
pocket ; and many a time has he been punished
for drawing on the walls of the schoolroom. In
fact he cannot resist a whitewashed wall. One da
this boy had the impudence to draw a caricature
of an old man, a bell-ringer of the village church,
in the belfry of the church itself. There you see
him in the picture drawing away, and evidently

pleased with his own work. The old man went to
the rector to complain, who was very angry; but

of course went to see the caricature, and came away
laughing.

Little Milly and her papa are having a game before nurse fetches her to go to bed. Every evening
down comes Milly before papa's late dinner, and
after he has told her two or three stories, she has a
ride upon his knee. He gets quite out of breath,
and his little girl too, before the ride is over ; but

it is a pretty sight to see papa and Milly playing
together. She sings :

> Ride a cock horse to Banbury Cross,
> To see an old lady get on a white horse.
> Rings on her fingers, bells on her toes ;
> She shall have music wherever she goes.

Milly's hair flies out as she rides, and her little
face is all rosy and dimpled. At last comes a knock
at the door ; and nurse appears for Miss Milly to
go to Bedfordshire.

We had a picture before of one of these St. Bernard
dogs saving a little boy from the snow. Here we

have two of them, out in a terrible storm, scraping
away the snow from a poor traveller, who has been
buried in it.

Look at these cottage children playing by a pond!
How happy they appear! That little bit of wood
with a paper sail seems an excellent toy-boat to

them who have never had a better, and the boys
find it fun to wade into the water. Meanwhile the
girls take care of baby, and Pincher, the steady
old doggie, looks after them all.

This is also a scene of country life. Here are some woodcutters resting from their work, while some of the trees they have felled are being drawn away by a team of fine strong horses. The beautiful trees that have so often given shade in

summer, are going to be useful in other ways. Some will be cut into logs to make bright fires. Some will go to build ships, some houses, but never to make anything more beautiful than the grand trees themselves were, as they stood waving in the wind.

How cleverly this dear little girl is doing up her hair in nice neat plaits! She is kind and good too, I am sure, because she is very fond

of flowers and birds. Look how tame the dear little dicky is, perched there upon her looking-glass, singing his morning song to her while she dresses!

Yes, Johnny, this is cricket, as you say; and these boys seem to be having a famous game. The ground is nice and smooth, the weather fine, they have their tent pitched, and the players are all in proper cricketing dress. It is a merry scene. The batsmen stand ready to send the

ball flying through the air; and then how they will start off running backwards and forwards, and count ever so many runs! A fine old English game, children, is this same game of Cricket. I trust my little Johnny will some day be a good cricketer. Indeed, I hope he will be good at all sorts of exercises, and grow up a fine strong man.

G

I am afraid this boy has been very naughty, for look how angry his mamma is with him! I think I can tell what has happened. You see that broken vase upon the ground? Well, I suspect he has knocked it off the table with his ball, and

then has denied it, and said the dog had knocked it down. But his mamma sees through it all; she would have forgiven him easily for breaking the vase, but now she is seriously angry, and grieved too, to find that he has told her a falsehood.

Here we have another mamma who is displeased with her children, but not so seriously, I think, as the poor mother in the last picture. I fancy that this little boy and girl have been quarrelling, and mamma calls them to her, and gives them both a

lecture, telling them that such discord in a family destroys all happiness, and that it arises from selfishness in each of them. Gently and kindly she speaks; but I am sure she feels very sad to think that her little ones, who might be so happy, make their own misery by quarrelling.

What is this you bring me, Johnny dear? Oh, I see; this is a race-course. The course is being cleared, for the horses are going to start; and this man rides along to give notice. There is a stupid

old cow just running across the ground: some dogs, too, have to be whipped out of the way. But though all is noise and confusion now, in another minute the course will be cleared for the race.

How fond you are of horses, Johnny! This is
a hunting scene you bring me now. The hounds
and hunters have evidently lost their fox, and this
gentleman is asking a countryman if he has seen

it. While he speaks, Mr. Foxy himself comes
stealing out from the brushwood close to them.
But the hounds are not near, nor on the scent,
so I think poor Foxy will probably manage to
escape.

This is little Tommy Titmouse coming in to say
"Good night" to papa and mamma. It is almost
his first attempt at walking; and partly by sup-

porting himself on dear old Carlo's nose, and
partly by the help of nurse, he gets on very well,
you see.

Look at Willie Danvers bounding along over the stepping-stones!   To think that once he could walk no better than little Tommy Titmouse!   He

has stopped on his way from school to pick some sweet wild flowers for his mother, who is ill : now he is running home as fast as he can.

Cissy dear, this is a very pretty picture you
have chosen.   Here is a handsome young couple,
dressed as people used to dress a hundred years
ago, walking arm-in-arm upon a terrace.   What
shall we suppose them to be ?   Shall they be

people of the present day dressed up in fancy
dresses ?   That will hardly do ; for they are evidently not at a fancy ball.   Let us suppose them
to be two nice little people, who lived long ago,
and walked and talked together in those days as
they might now.   We will suppose, too, if you like,
that they were going to be married ; and let us
hope that they were happy.

Here's a queer-looking figure: how very long and thin! I wonder if he ever eats any dinner! But we ought not to laugh at a poor man who

looks as if he were starving. Is he a poet who can't sell his rhymes; or a schoolmaster who has no pupils, I wonder? I cannot make him out for certain, but paste him into the book all the same.

Oh, I have something funny to tell you about
this sketch. It is a portrait of Elfie, our old Skye
terrier, which papa made a long time ago. Elfie
was ordered to sit up and beg, as you see him
doing in the sketch, and was scolded once or twice

for moving. When papa had finished, we all went
to luncheon, forgetting poor dear old Elfie. An
hour afterwards we came back into the drawing-
room, and there was Elfie, in exactly the same
position, looking very miserable, but still waiting
for permission to get down. Dear old doggie!

You have managed to find a very nice picture for your scrap-book, Lily dear: two little shepherd-boys playing away on their pipes, while they

watch the sheep! Their hats are decked with wild flowers; the lark sings in the sky, joining the concert; the sheep turn round to listen; and boys, birds, and sheep are all merry together.

This is a lady who thinks her figure shows to advantage in the game of croquet.   She is called

Aunt Barbara by her nephews and nieces, who laugh at her among themselves ; but they don't laugh at her to her face, for she is a rich old maid. The youngest of her nieces, little Barbara, her

godchild, did tell her once she was too fat to play
at croquet. The old lady, though very good-

natured generally, is sudden in wrath, and, but for
the interference of Sambo, the black footman, little
Barbara would have felt the weight of her aunt's
fat hand.

This picture shows us one of those contrasts which, when seen in real life, are very, very sad to witness. I do not know the story of the picture, but I should think the scene is meant for Ireland. We have the great house and the hovel side by

side. A richly-dressed little child is riding his fat pony, with an overfed and pampered spaniel waddling beside him. On the other side of a little stream we see childhood also; but childhood shorn of its beauty, gaiety, and grace, by the sufferings of extreme poverty. It is a terrible difference.

Here is another hunting scene for you, Johnny.
Here the fox has been lost; or, perhaps, they have
not found in this covert, and are going to try some-

where else. The huntsman is blowing his horn, to
get the hounds together, while the whipper-in flogs
the stragglers who are lingering behind. Look
how eager the horses appear! They are just as
eager as the men are for the sport to begin.

How can this good boy and girl learn their lessons with that tiresome little brat of a brother in the room ? He is too young to learn lessons himself, and wants the others to be always playing

with him. Look what he is doing now. He has put on his big brother's cap, strapped his knapsack on to his own shoulders, taken the slate and books off the table, and pretends he is going off to school. The brother and sister laugh heartily, but how can they learn their lessons ?

This lady must be going away on a journey.
She is just giving the children into nurse's charge

before she says good-bye to their grandpapa. Her
last words to her children are : " My darlings, pray
be good, and always love each other."

H

So Johnny has found the pretty sketch that papa made long ago of poor old Harkaway, his favourite hunter, and Columbine, the old hound he petted so much. Ah! dear children, both these faithful creatures died before you were born; but you know the large picture in the dining-room—the

full length of Harkaway—that dear papa painted? Well, this sketch is a study of the heads of Harkaway and Columbine, made before the picture was begun. The horse was old when I married your papa: he was past work, and used to live quite an idle life. He passed his days out in the large field, and at night was put into a comfortable shed with plenty of nice warm straw. But, although he had become quite feeble, with bent knees, and shaky legs, I believe he would still have followed the hounds, if he had been allowed. There is another sketch somewhere, which papa made of Harkaway when he was quite old. Ah, here it is! This is

just as papa saw him one day, when the hounds and huntsmen were passing through the next field. He was looking over the gate, trembling all over with excitement; his eyes sparkling, and nostrils distended.

This is little Mary Manly; a good little girl.
Her father works hard in the fields, while her

mother takes care of the cottage. Mary helps
mother as much as she can; she wishes she were
big and strong enough to help in washing.

But we see here that Mary is of use to her mo ther sometimes ; and then she feels quite happy.

They are washing up the things together after dinner : she works away like a little woman, drying the plates as mother takes them from the water.

Next-comes a picture of three little-sparrows perched upon a branch. I will tell you what they remind me of. Do you remember, when we used to hang out the canary in the garden last summer,

how the sparrows always collected about him. How they pecked at his sugar, and watercress, and even got at his seed sometimes! And when they perched upon his cage, how angry Topaz was, and how he pecked at their claws! If anyone went by, they only retreated to the nearest branches, and perched there like those in the picture.

My Lily brings me another bird picture. This
represents a great blue and yellow macaw, with a

loud harsh voice, and splendid plumage. Macaws
are very large parrots, and several are to be seen
at the Zoological Gardens, where they almost
deafen you with their noise.

Here has been a dreadful storm : some of the plants are blown down, and the garden walk is like a stream of water. It is in France, and these two

boys have borrowed some wooden shoes, such as the peasants wear, that they may have the fun of running about in all the wet. As they run, the wooden shoes fly off, for they are much too big.

These little girls have come to get water for
their thirsty flowers, for each has a little garden of

her own. One works hard at the pump, while the
other holds the cans.

Here we have a pleasant sociable tea-party. These little people are Rosy and Maude Drummond, but they call themselves just now Mrs. Jones and Mrs. Smith. They meet at tea at Miss Penelope Prim's; that lady being the big doll,

seated on the easy chair in the middle. Mrs. Smith and Mrs. Jones have each brought a child, and the conversation between them is often interrupted by the slaps and shakes they have to give their little ones, who, I grieve to say, bleed a great deal of sawdust. Miss Penelope all the time sits smiling there, without either joining in the conversation, or partaking of tea.

This is a picture of Mrs. Tabbyskin. See how
gentle and sweet-tempered she seems, seated on

the edge of that great stone vase! She is purring
away, and ready to play with anybody. Gentle
Mrs. Tabbyskin, who could help liking you!

Oh, Mrs. Tabbyskin, Mrs. Tabbyskin! who could like you now? How different you seemed in the last picture. Cruel cat, to kill that dear little

bird! The poor thing is dead now, so it can no longer feel your sharp teeth and claws; and I suppose you will set to work to eat it. But we shall no longer care to play with you, nor think you good and gentle.

Really, Mrs. Tabbyskin, you do not improve upon more intimate acquaintance. Although you are now attacking one of your own size and kind, which is better than killing a dear little bird, still

you look so ugly and vicious, with your glaring eyes, flattened ears, and open mouth, that I for one could never pet you again. The pretty white cat does not look half so savage. Good-bye, Mrs. Tabbyskin, and we don't want to see you again.

This woman has been haymaking, as we may see by her rake. She has had her baby out in the

field with her all day, and now she carries him home in a basket on her back. I think baby is enjoying his ride.

My little Lily has picked out a picture of a merry party for her scrap-book. What a set of jolly tars to be sure! I think they have just come on shore, and are having a friendly glass together, before they separate to go to their different homes. Perhaps they have been away for many, many

months, perhaps even for years, so you may think how glad these honest fellows must be to reach their native land again. Think, too, how eagerly their wives and children must be looking for them, after all these months of anxiety, when the poor women have quaked and trembled at every gale of wind. I hope our jolly tars will not sit long over their parting glass, but hurry home to their wives.

Oh, look at this monkey! How he hangs by his tail while he stretches out his arms to get the apples from the box below! What a queer-

looking fellow he is! You say you would like to have a monkey, Cissy? I think, dear, you would soon wish him away again.

What good little children we have here to be
sure! They are Tommy and Jane Goodheart,
and are spending the day with grandmamma, who
is very old, and cannot bear fatigue or noise.

They understand this, and give her as little trouble
as possible. While Tommy is looking at a picture-
book in her lap, she drops off into a comfortable
nap. He still looks at his book, but takes care not
to disturb her; while little Janie, who is amusing
herself with pictures too, is as quiet as a mouse.

I

This picture shows us a pretty little girl who is going to a Christmas party, but I am afraid she thinks too much about her dress. The night

before the party she cannot sleep for thinking of her dress, and gets up in the middle of the night to look at it in the wardrobe. I like her better in the next picture—for we will suppose this to be

the same little girl. Let us say that she is a
country clergyman's daughter, and here she has

come to see a sick boy, the son of poor cottagers,
and has brought him from her mamma a basket
full of nice nourishing things to eat.

So, Lily, you have found another picture representing one of Æsop's fables : that of the Hare and the Hound.   I will tell you the fable.   Once upon a time a hound started a hare, and tried to

catch him ; but after running a long way, gave up the chase.   A shepherd, who happened to be near when the hound stopped, laughed at him, saying : " The hare runs faster than you can."   To which the hound replied : " You do not see the difference between us : I was only running for a dinner, he for his life."

Well, Cissy darling, I think you have given me now one of the prettiest pictures we shall have in the scrap-book. Here you see are four dear little children playing in the fields. It is a bright summer's day, but the sun is just going down, so the little people may venture out with bare heads

Still there are butterflies about, one can tell, for the children have nets to catch them. True, we cannot see any butterflies, as you say, Johnny dear; and I rather doubt if the children can. either. However, they seem happy and good skipping and dancing through the long grass and well taken care of, we may be sure, by their faithful doggie.

This is a beautiful Newfoundland dog, and very much like our Neptune, whom you have heard of, children, though he died years ago. The great

exploit of Neptune's life was his saving that of a tipsy soldier, who fell off the pier at Portsmouth. Papa sent Neptune in after him, and the brave, strong dog brought the man to shore.

See what busy little people we have here! what are they about? You think, Johnny, that they are having a doll's tea-party? Silly little man! where are the tea-things? as Lily wisely asks. Well, Lily dear, give us *your* opinion on the subject. You think they are teaching lessons to their dolls?

Johnny says: "Toopid, where are the books?" True, Johnny, though not politely remarked. What do *you* say, Cissy? You think they are mending their dolls? You are right, dear, and I will give you a rhyme I have heard:

> See how good and clever also
> Children, when they like, can be;
> Mending dollies' clothes and bodies,
> Working hard, as you may see.

But, dear, dear, what is this! Why we have come to the end of our Scrap-book: we have only room for one little picture more. Well, we must find a pretty one that will fit in nicely. Ah! I think my little Lily has found the very thing—a pretty little girl with a book open upon her knees! One might almost fancy this picture was intended to represent our Lily herself looking at her Scrap-book.

J. OGDEN AND CO., PRINTERS, 172, ST. JOHN STREET, E.C.

GEORGE ROUTLEDGE & SONS'

CATALOGUE OF

A THOUSAND

JUVENILE BOOKS

Reward and Gift Books

AND

CHILDREN'S PICTURE BOOKS.

"No firm surpasses Messrs. Routledge in Sixpenny and Shilling Picture Story-Books. Could not be better drawn, printed, or coloured, if they cost twenty shillings, instead of twelve pence."—*Standard*, December 23, 1870.

LONDON : THE BROADWAY, LUDGATE.
NEW YORK : 416, BROOME STREET.

August, 1875.

CONTENTS.

SEVEN-AND-SIXPENNY BOOKS, *continued.*

s. d.

7 6 **Bonnechose's France.** A New Edition. 1872.

The Language of Flowers. By the Rev. ROBERT TYAS. With 12 pages of Coloured Plates by KRONHEIM.

Longfellow's Poetical Works. With Plates by JOHN GILBERT. Author's Complete Edition. Demy 8vo, cloth, gilt edges.

Bunyan's Pilgrim's Progress. With 100 Plates by J. D. WATSON.

Popular Natural History. By the Rev. J. G. WOOD, M.A. With Hundreds of Illustrations.

National Nursery Rhymes. Set to Music by J. W. ELLIOTT. With Original Illustrations, engraved by DALZIEL Brothers.

Naomi; or, The Last Days of Jerusalem. By Mrs. WEBB. With Steel Plates. Post 8vo, cloth, gilt edges.

Dante's Divine Comedy. Translated by H. W. LONGFELLOW. 1 vol., crown 8vo, cloth.

Hogg on the Microscope. With 500 Illustrations and 8 Coloured Plates.

Andersen's Stories for the Household. 8vo, cloth, gilt edges, with 220 Illustrations.

Robinson Crusoe. With 110 Plates by J. D. WATSON.

Sheridan Knowles' Dramatic Works.

In cloth, gilt edges, **6s.** each.

6 0 **Routledge's Every Boy's Annual for 1876.** Edited by EDMUND ROUTLEDGE. With many Illustrations, and beautiful Coloured Plates.

Shipwrecks and Disasters at Sea. By W. H. G. KINGSTON. With more than 100 Illustrations.

The Adventures of Robinson Playfellow, a Young French Marine. With 24 Plates, and many Woodcuts.

Bab Ballads. By W. S. GILBERT. With Illustrations by the Author.

Travelling About. By Lady BARKER. With Six Plates and 5 Maps.

Pepper's Boy's Play-book of Science. 400 Plates.

D'Aulnoy's Fairy Tales. Translated by PLANCHÉ.

Perrault's Fairy Tales. Translated by PLANCHÉ, &c.

Pepper's Play-book of Mines, Minerals, and Metals. With 300 Illustrations. Post 8vo, gilt.

SIX-SHILLING BOOKS, *continued.*

s. d.

Motley's Rise of the Dutch Republic. Crown 8vo, 6 o
cloth, gilt.

An Illustrated Natural History. By the Rev. J. G.
WOOD, M.A. 500 Illustrations.

The Playfellow. By HARRIET MARTINEAU. With
Coloured Plates.

The English at the North Pole. By JULES VERNÉ.
129 Illustrations by RIOU.

The Field of Ice. By JULES VERNÉ. 129 Illustrations by RIOU.

The Adventures of Johnny Ironsides. 115 Plates.

ROUTLEDGE'S BRITISH POETS.

EDITED BY REV. R. A. WILLMOTT.

Illustrated by BIRKET FOSTER, Sir JOHN GILBERT, &c.

Chaucer's Canterbury Tales. Illustrated by 5 o
CORBOULD.

Kirke White. Illustrated by BIRKET FOSTER.

Southey's Joan of Arc, and Minor Poems.

Herbert. With Life and Notes by the Rev. R. A.
WILLMOTT.

Longfellow's Complete Poetical Works. With
Illustrations. Fcap. 8vo.

Burns' Poetical Works. Illustrated by JOHN
GILBERT.

Fairfax's Tasso's Jerusalem Delivered. Illustrated by CORBOULD.

Crabbe. Illustrated by BIRKET FOSTER.

Moore's Poems. Illustrated by CORBOULD, &c.

Byron's Poems. Illustrated by GILBERT, WOLF,
FOSTER, &c.

Campbell's Poetical Works. Illustrated by W.
HARVEY.

Lover's Poetical Works. With a Portrait.

Rogers' Poetical Works. With a Portrait.

Dryden's Poetical Works. With a Portrait, &c.

Mrs. Hemans' Poems.

Lord Lytton's Poetical Works.

Lord Lytton's Dramatic Works.

ROUTLEDGE'S FIVE-SHILLING JUVENILE BOOKS.

In fcap. 8vo and post 8vo, gilt, Illustrated by GILBERT, HARVEY, FOSTER, and ZWECKER.

s. d.

5 0 Children of the New Forest. By *Marryat.*

Little Savage. By *Marryat.*

History of British India.

Lilian's Golden Hours. By *Silverpen.*

Boy's Treasury of Sports and Pastimes.

The Queens of Society.

The Wits and Beaux of Society.

Entertaining Knowledge.

Pleasant Tales.

Extraordinary Men and Women.

Dora and her Papa. *Author of "Lilian's Golden Hours."*

Great Battles of the British Army.

The Prince of the House of David.

The Pillar of Fire.

The Throne of David.

The Story of the Reformation. By *D'Aubigné.*

Popular Astronomy and Orbs of Heaven.

Once upon a Time. By *Charles Knight.*

White's History of England.

The Winborough Boys. By *Rev. H. C. Adams.*

The Prairie Bird. By *Hon. C. Murray.*

The Great Sieges of History. With Coloured Plates.

Cooper's Leatherstocking Tales.

Great Battles of the British Navy. With Coloured Plates.

Memoirs of Great Commanders. With Coloured Plates.

The Family Arabian Nights. Coloured Plates.

The Adventures of Robin Hood. With Coloured Plates.

Holiday Stories. By *Lady Barker.*

Half Hours with the Best Letter Writers. By *C. Knight.*

Characteristics of Women. By *Mrs. Jameson.*

Memoirs of Celebrated Female Sovereigns. By Mrs. *Jameson.*

What Men have said about Woman.

British Heroes in Foreign Wars. By *James Grant.* With Coloured Plates.

Don Quixote for Boys. With Coloured Plates by Kronheim.

Wroxby College. By *Rev. H. C. Adams.*

Boys. By *Lady Barker.*

Sunday Evenings at Home By *Rev. H. C. Adams, M.A.* First Series.

—— Second Series.

Memoirs of Celebrated Women. By *G. P. R. James.*

Nine Little Goslings. By *Susan Coolidge.* With Illustrations.

ROUTLEDGE'S FIVE-SHILLING BOOKS.

s. d.

Little Wide-Awake for 1876. By Mrs. SALE 5 0
BARKER. With 400 Illustrations and Coloured Frontispiece.

Grimm's Fairy Tales. With Coloured Plates.
Crown 8vo, gilt.

Hans Andersen's Stories and Tales. 80 Illustrations, and Coloured Plates.

Walter Crane's Picture Book. With 64 pages of
Coloured Plates. Cloth, gilt edges.

Country Life. Illustrated by Poetry, and 40 Pictures
by BIRKET FOSTER.

What the Moon Saw, and other Tales. By HANS C.
ANDERSEN. With 80 Illustrations, and Coloured Plates.

Chimes and Rhymes for Youthful Times. With
Coloured Plates. (Uniform with " Schnick-Schnack.")

Buds and Flowers. A Coloured Book for Children.
(Uniform with " Schnick-Schnack.") Small 4to, cloth.

Schnick-Schnack. Trifles for the Little Ones. With
Coloured Plates. Small 4to, cloth.

Buttercups and Daisies. A new Coloured Book for
Children. (Uniform with " Schnick-Schnack.") Small 4to, cloth.

Watts' Divine and Moral Songs. With 108 Woodcuts, engraved by COOPER.

Original Poems for Infant Minds. By JANE and
A. TAYLOR. With Original Illustrations by the Best Artists, engraved by J. D. COOPER.

Little Lays for Little Folk. Selected by J. G.
WATTS. With Original Illustrations by the best living Artists,
engraved by J. D. COOPER. 4to, cloth, gilt edges.

The Picture Book of Reptiles, Fishes, and In-
sects. By the Rev J. G. WOOD, M.A. With 250 Illustrations.
4to, cloth.

——————— **Birds.** By the Rev. J. G.
WOOD, M.A. With 242 Illustrations. 4to, cloth.

——————— **Mammalia.** By the Rev. J.
G. WOOD, M.A. With 250 Illustrations. 4to, cloth.

Happy Day Stories for the Young. By Dr.
DULCKEN. With full-page Plates by A. B. HOUGHTON.

ROUTLEDGE'S FIVE-SHILLING BOOKS.

In super-royal 8vo, cloth gilt, price 5s.

s. d.

5 0 **Walter Crane's Picture Book.** Containing 64 pages of Pictures, designed by WALTER CRANE, viz.:—"Luckieboy's Party," "The Old Courtier," "How Jessie was Lost," "The Fairy Ship," "Chattering," "Annie and Jack in London," "Grammar in Rhyme," "The Multiplication Table in Verse."

Walter Crane's New Toy Book. Containing 64 pages of Pictures, designed by WALTER CRANE, viz.:—"Cinderella," "My Mother," "The Forty Thieves," "The Three Bears," "One, Two, Buckle my Shoe," "Puffy," "This Little Pig," "Noah's Ark A B C."

Goody Two-Shoes Picture Book. Containing "Goody Two-Shoes," "Beauty and the Beast," "A B C of Old Friends," and "The Frog Prince." With 24 pages of Coloured Plates from designs by WALTER CRANE.

The Henny-Penny Picture Book. Containing "Henny-Penny," "Sleeping Beauty," "Baby" and "The Peacock at Home." With 24 pages of Coloured Plates.

The Poll Parrot Picture Book. Containing "Tittums and Fido," "Reynard the Fox," "Anne and her Mamma," and "The Cats' Tea Party."

Routledge's Coloured A B C Book. Containing "The Alphabet of Fairy Tales," "The Farm Yard Alphabet," "Alphabet of Flowers," and "Tom Thumb's Alphabet."

My Mother's Picture Book. Containing "My Mother," "The Dogs' Dinner Party," "Little Dog Trusty," and "The White Cat." Large 4to, cloth.

The Red Riding-Hood Picture Book. Containing "Red Riding Hood," "Three Bears," "Three Kittens," and "Dash and the Ducklings." Large 4to, cloth.

Our Nurse's Picture Book. Containing "Tom Thumb," "Babes in the Wood," "Jack and the Beanstalk," and "Puss in Boots." Large quarto, cloth.

The Child s Picture Book of Domestic Animals. 12 Large Plates, printed in Colours by KRONHEIM. Large oblong, cloth.

The Child's Picture Book of Wild Animals. 12 Large Plates, printed in Colours by KRONHEIM. Large oblong, cloth.

Pictures from English History. 63 Coloured Plates by KRONHEIM. Demy 4to, cloth.

FIVE-SHILLING BOOKS, *continued.*

s. d.

Routledge's Scripture Gift Book. Containing "The 5 0 Old Testament Alphabet," "The New Testament Alphabet," "The History of Moses," and "The History of Joseph." Demy 4to, cloth.

Routledge's Picture Gift Book. Containing "Nursery Songs," "Alphabet of Trades," "Nursery Tales," and "This Little Pig."

The Pet Lamb Picture Book. Containing "The Toy Primer," "The Pet Lamb," "The Fair One with Golden Locks," and "Jack the Giant Killer."

The Robinson Crusoe Picture Book. Containing "Robinson Crusoe," "Cock Sparrow," "Queer Characters," and "Æsop's Fables."

ROUTLEDGE'S FOUR-AND-SIXPENNY JUVENILES.

A New Series of Juvenile Works.

All well Illustrated, and bound in an entirely New Binding, expressly designed for them.

LIST OF THE SERIES.

Life of Richelieu. By *W. Robson.*

Monarchs of the Main. By *Walter Thornbury.*

Roger Kyffyn's Ward. By *W. H. G. Kingston.*

The Man o' War's Bell. By *Lieut. C. R. Low.*

The Orville College Boys. By *Mrs. Henry Wood.*

Wonderful Inventions. By *John Timbs*

Æsop's Fables. With Plates by *H. Weir.*

The Illustrated Girl's Own Treasury.

The Boy's Own Country 4 6 Book. By *Miller.*

The Forest Ranger. By *Major Campbell.*

Pleasures of Old Age.

Tales upon Texts. By the *Rev. H. C. Adams.*

Pictures from Nature. By *Mary Howitt.*

Stephen Scudamore the Younger. By *A. Locker.*

Hunting Grounds of the Old World.

Watch the End. By *Thomas Miller.*

In fcap. 8vo, cloth, gilt edges, price 4s. each.

Every Girl's Book. By Miss LAWFORD. With many 4 0 Illustrations.

Every Little Boy's Book. By EDMUND ROUTLEDGE. With many Illustrations.

ROUTLEDGE'S THREE-AND-SIXPENNY REWARD BOOKS.

With Coloured Illustrations, gilt sides.

s. d.

3 6 Robinson Crusoe.
Sandford and Merton.
Evenings at Home.
Swiss Family Robinson.
Edgeworth's Popular Tales.
———— Moral Tales.
———— Parent's Assistant.
———— Early Lessons.
The Old Helmet. By the *Author of "The Wide, Wide World."*
The Wide, Wide World.
Edgar Clifton.

The Lamplighter.
Melbourne House.
Queechy.
Ellen Montgomery's Book-shelf.
The Two Schoolgirls.
The Pilgrim's Progress.
Gulliver's Travels.
Andersen's Fairy Tales.
The Arabian Nights.
The Adventures of Robin Hood.
Don Quixote for Boys.
Captain Cook's Voyages.

All the above have Coloured Plates.

MAYNE REID'S JUVENILE BOOKS.

In fcap. 8vo, cloth gilt, with Illustrations.

3 6 Bruin.
The Boy Tar.
The Desert Home.
Odd People.
Ran away to Sea.
The Forest Exiles.
The Young Yägers.

The Young Voyageurs.
The Plant Hunters.
The Quadroon.
The War Trail.
The Bush Boys.
The Boy Hunters.

ANNE BOWMAN'S JUVENILE BOOKS.

With Plates, fcap. 8vo, cloth gilt.

3 6 The Boy Voyagers.
The Castaways.
The Young Nile Voyagers.
The Boy Pilgrims.
The Boy Foresters.
Tom and the Crocodiles.
Esperanza.

The Young Exiles.
The Bear Hunters.
The Kangaroo Hunters.
Young Yachtsmen.
Among the Tartar Tents.
Clarissa.
How to make the Best of It.

ROUTLEDGE'S

THREE-AND-SIXPENNY JUVENILE BOOKS.

With Engravings, cloth gilt.

s. d.
3 6

Sketches and Anecdotes of Animal Life. By *Rev. J. G. Wood.*

Grimm's Home Stories.

Animal Traits and Characteristics. By *Rev. J. G. Wood.*

My Feathered Friends. By *Rev. J. G. Wood.*

Schoolboy Honour. By *Rev. H. C. Adams.*

Red Eric. By *R. M. Ballantyne.*

Louis' School-Days.

Wild Man of the West. By *Ballantyne.*

Dashwood Priory. By *E. J. May.*

Freaks on the Fells. By *R. M. Ballantyne.*

Lamb's Tales from Shakspeare.

Balderscourt; or, Holiday Tales By *Rev. H. C. Adams.*

Rob Roy. By *James Grant.*

Johnny Jordan. By *Mrs. Eiloart.*

Ernie Elton, at Home and at School.

Lost Among the Wild Men.

Percy's Tales of the Kings of England.

Boys of Beechwood. By *Mrs. Eiloart.*

Papa's Wise Dogs.

Digby Heathcote. By *Kingston.*

Hawthorne's Wonder Book.

Will Adams. By *Dalton.*

Little Ladders to Learning. 1st series.

Ditto. 2nd series.

White's Selborne. 200 Cuts.

Boyhood of Great Men.

Footprints of Famous Men. By *J. G. Edgar.*

Rev. J. G. Wood's Boy's Own Natural History Book.

Tales of Charlton School. By the *Rev. H. C. Adams.*

Our Domestic Pets. By *Rev. J. G. Wood.*

History for Boys. By *J. G. Edgar.*

Saxelford. By *E. J. May.*

Old Tales for the Young.

Harry Hope's Holiday.

Boy Life Among the Indians.

Old Saws new Set. By the *Author of "A Trap to Catch a Sunbeam."*

Hollowdell Grange.

Mayhew's Wonders of Science.

Peasant - Boy Philosopher.

Barford Bridge. By the *Rev. H. C. Adams.*

The White Brunswickers. By *Rev. H. C. Adams.*

A Boy's Adventures in the Wilds of Australia. By *W. Howitt.*

Tales of Walter's School Days. By *Rev. H. C. Adams.*

The Path She Chose. By *F. M. S.*

The Gates Ajar.

A Country Life. By *W. Howitt.*

Stories for Sundays. By *Rev. H. C. Adams.*

THREE-AND-SIXPENNY JUVENILE BOOKS, *continued.*

s. d.

3 6 The Child's Country Book. By *T. Miller.* Coloured Plates.

The Child's Story Book. By *T. Miller.* Coloured Plates.

Uncle Tom's Cabin.

Tom Dunstone's Troubles. By *Mrs. Eiloart.*

The Young Marooners.

Influence. By the *Author of " A Trap to Catch a Sunbeam."*

Jack of the Mill. By *W. Howitt.*

Dick Rodney. By *James Grant.*

Jack Manly. By *James Grant.*

Sybil's Friend. By *Florence Marryat.*

Life in the Red Brigade. By *R. M. Ballantyne.*

Edgar Clifton.

Stepping Heavenward, and Aunt Jane's Hero.

Valentin. By *Henry Kingsley.*

With a Stout Heart. By *Mrs. Sale Barker.*

Opening a Chestnut Burr. By the *Rev. C. P. Roe.*

What Might Have been Expected.

Tales of Nethercourt. By *Rev. H. C. Adams.*

THE GOLDEN RULE LIBRARY FOR YOUNG LADIES.

In cloth gilt, post 8vo, with full-page Illustrations, price 3s. 6d. each.

3 6 The Four Sisters.

The Golden Rule.

Lillieslea.

The Village Idol.

The Doctor's Ward.

Through Life and for Life.

Tell Mamma.

Little Women.

Heroines of History.

Heroines of Domestic Life.

What Can She Do?

Barriers Burned Away.

The Girls' Birthday Book.

Blanche and Beryl.

Miss Roberts' Fortune.

In post 8vo, cloth, 3s. 6d. each.

THE FOUQUÉ FAIRY LIBRARY.

A Collection of DE LA MOTTE FOUQUÉ'S most Popular Fairy Tales, Illustrated by TENNIEL, SELOUS, and others.

3 6 The Four Seasons.

Romantic Fiction.

The Magic Ring. *Other Vols. to follow.*

ROUTLEDGE'S ALBUM SERIES.

In cloth gilt, price 3s. 6d., beautifully printed on toned paper.   *s. d.*

Otto Speckter's Fables. With 100 Coloured Plates. 3 6
A New Edition. 4to, cloth, gilt edges.

Routledge's Sunday Album for Children. With 80 Plates by J. D. WATSON, Sir JOHN GILBERT, and others.

The Boys' and Girls' Illustrated Gift-Book. With many Illustrations by McCONNELL, WEIR, and others.

The Child's Picture Fable Book. With 60 Plates by HARRISON WEIR.

The Coloured Album for Children. With 72 Pages of Coloured Plates.

The Picture Book of the Sagacity of Animals. With 60 Plates by HARRISON WEIR.

For a Good Child. Containing "The Alphabet of Trades," "The Cats' Tea-Party," and "Cinderella." With 18 Pages of Coloured Plates.

Routledge's Picture Book. Containing "The Farm Yard Alphabet," "The Alphabet of Flowers," and "The Pretty Name Alphabet." With 18 Pages of Coloured Plates.

A Present for My Darling. Containing "This Little Pig went to Market," "Nursery Tales," and "Tom Thumb's Alphabet." With 18 Pages of Coloured Plates.

The Good Child's Album. Containing "Red Riding-Hood," "Mother Hubbard and Cock Robin," and "The Three Kittens." With 18 Pages of Coloured Plates.

Nursery Rhymes. With Plates by H. S. MARKS.

Nursery Songs. With Plates by H. S. MARKS.

The Child's Coloured Gift-Book. With 72 Coloured Plates.

The Child's Coloured Scripture Book. With 72 Coloured Plates.

The Nursery Album. 72 Pages of Coloured Plates.

The Golden Harp Album. With 400 Illustrations.

Happy Child Life. With 24 Pages of Coloured Plates.

Album for Children. With 180 page Plates by MILLAIS, Sir JOHN GILBERT, and others. Imp. 16mo, cloth.

Popular Nursery Tales. With 180 Illustrations by J. D. WATSON and others. Imp. 16mo, cloth.

Child's Picture Story Book. With 180 Plates, Imp. 16mo, cloth.

A Picture Story Book. Containing "King Nutcracker," and other Tales. 300 Illustrations. Imp. 16mo, cloth.

The Book of Trades. By THOMAS ARCHER.

s. d.

3 6 Mixing in Society. A Complete Manual of Manners.

The Children's Bible Book. With 100 Illustrations, engraved by DALZIEL.

A Handy History of England for the Young. With 120 Illustrations, engraved by DALZIEL.

Griset's Grotesques. With Rhymes by TOM HOOD. Fancy boards.

The Children's Poetry Book. With 16 Coloured Plates. Square, cloth.

Out of the Heart: Spoken to the Little Ones. By HANS ANDERSEN. With 16 Coloured Plates. Cloth.

The Nursery Picture Book. With 630 Illustrations. Folio, boards.

ROUTLEDGE'S COLOURED PICTURE BOOKS.

In super-royal 8vo, cloth gilt, price 3s. 6d. each, or mounted on linen, 5s. each.

THIRD SERIES, *containing*

Happy Days of Childhood.	Hop o' My Thumb.
Sing a Song of Sixpence. *This is not kept on Linen.*	Gaping, Wide-Mouthed, Waddling Frog.

ANIMALS AND BIRDS, *containing*

Wild Animals.	British Animals.
Parrots.	Singing Birds.

BOOK OF ALPHABETS, *containing*

The Railroad Alphabet.	The Sea-Side Alphabet.
The Good Boys' and Girls' Alphabet.	The Farm-Yard Alphabet.

KING LUCKIEBOY'S PICTURE BOOK, *containing*

King Luckieboy's Party.	The Old Courtier.
This Little Pig went to Market.	Picture Book of Horses.

OUR PETS' PICTURE BOOK, *containing*

The History of Our Pets.	Aladdin.
Nursery Rhymes.	Noah's Ark A B C.

THE MARQUIS OF CARABAS' PICTURE BOOK, with Designs by WALTER CRANE, *containing*

Puss in Boots.	Old Mother Hubbard.
The Absurd A B C.	Valentine and Orson.

ROUTLEDGE'S BRITISH POETS.

(3s. 6d. Editions.)

Elegantly printed on tinted paper, crown 8vo, gilt edges,
with Illustrations.

Those marked * can be had elegantly bound in IVORINE, price 7s. 6d.

s. d.
3 6

Longfellow. (Complete.)
Cowper.
Milton.
Wordsworth.
Southey.
Goldsmith.
* Kirke White.
Burns.
Moore.
Byron.
* Pope.
* James Montgomery.
Scott.
Herbert.
Campbell.
Bloomfield.
Shakspere.
* Chaucer.
Sacred Poems.
Choice Poems.
Shakspeare Gems.
Wit and Humour
Wise Sayings.
Longfellow's Dante—
    Paradiso.
————Purgatorio.
————Inferno.

* Lover's Poems.
Book of Familiar Quota-
    tions.
Bret Harte.
* Leigh Hunt.
* Dryden.
Ainsworth.
* Spenser.
* Rogers.
Mrs. Hemans.
Shelley.
Keats.
Coleridge.
L. E. L.
* Percy's Reliques.
* Dodd's Beauties of Shake-
    speare.
The Christian Year.
Keble.
E. Allan Poe.
Longfellow's Tales of a
    Wayside Inn. (Complete
    edition.)
————Prose Works.
The Mind of Shakespeare,
    as Exhibited in his Works.
The Comic Poets of the
    Nineteenth Century.

ROUTLEDGE'S STANDARD LIBRARY.

In post 8vo, toned paper, cloth, 3s. 6d. each.

3 6

The Arabian Nights.
Don Quixote.
Gil Blas.
Curiosities of Literature.
    By *Isaac D'Israeli*

1,001 Gems of British
    Poetry.
The Blackfriars Shak-
    spere. *Charles Knight.*
Cruden's Concordance.

STANDARD LIBRARY, *continued.*

s. d.

3 6 Boswell's Life of Johnson.
The Works of Oliver Goldsmith.
Routledge's Pronouncing Dictionary.
The Family Doctor.
Ten Thousand Wonderful Things.
Sterne's Works.
Extraordinary Popular Delusions.
Bartlett's Familiar Quotations.
The Spectator.
Routledge's Modern Speaker.
1,001 Gems of Prose.

Pope's Homer's Iliad and Odyssey.
Book of Modern Anecdotes. English, Irish, Scotch.
Josephus.
Book of Proverbs, Phrases, Quotations, and Mottoes.
The Book of Modern Anecdotes—Theatrical, Legal, and American.
The Book of Table Talk. By *W. C. Russell.*
Junius. (Woodfall's edition.)
Froissart's Chronicles.
Charles Lamb's Works. (Centenary edition.)

ROUTLEDGE'S THREE-SHILLING JUVENILES.

Under the above title Messrs. G. ROUTLEDGE & SONS *offer a New Series of Juvenile Books, all well Illustrated, and well bound in a New and Elegant Binding.*

LIST OF THE SERIES.

3 0 Dogs and their Ways. By *Williams.*
The Holiday Camp. By *St. John Corbet.*
Helen Mordaunt. By the *Author of "Naomi."*
Romance of Adventure.
Play Hours and Half Holidays. By *Rev. J. C. Atkinson.*
Walks and Talks of Two Schoolboys.
The Island Home.
Hildred the Daughter.
Hardy and Hunter.
Fred and the Gorillas. By *T. Miller.*
Frank Wildman's Adventures.

Wild Sports in the Far West.
Guizot's Moral Tales.
Voyage and Venture.
The Young Whaler. By *Gerstaecker.*
Great Cities of the Middle Ages.
Dawnings of Genius.
Celebrated Children.
Seven Wonders of the World.
Faery Gold. By *Henry Chorley.*
The Travels of Rolando.
Great Cities of the Ancient World.
Uncle Tom's Cabin for Children.

The Little Wide-Awake for 1876. By Mrs. SALE BARKER, with 400 Illustrations, fancy boards, 3*s.*

ROUTLEDGE'S ONE-SYLLABLE SERIES.

By MARY GODOLPHIN.

In 16mo, cloth gilt, with Coloured Plates, price 2s. 6d. each.

s. d.

Bunyan's Pilgrim's Progress.
Evenings at Home.

Swiss Family Robinson. 2 6
Child's First Lesson Book.

ROUTLEDGE'S HALF-CROWN JUVENILES.

Fcap. 8vo, Illustrated by the Best Artists, gilt, 2s. 6d. each.

Eda Morton and her Cousins. By *M. M. Bell.*
Gilbert the Adventurer.
The Lucky Penny, and other Tales. By *Mrs. S. C. Hall.*
Minna Raymond. Illustrated by B. FOSTER.
Helena Bertram. By the *Author of "The Four Sisters."*
Heroes of the Workshop, &c. By *E. L. Brightwell.*
Sunshine and Cloud. By *Miss Bowman.*
The Maze of Life. By the *Author of "The Four Sisters."*
The Wide, Wide World.
The Lamplighter. By *Cummins.*
The Rector's Daughter. By *Miss Bowman.*
The Old Helmet. By *Miss Wetherell.*
The Secret of a Life.
Queechy. By *Miss Wetherell.*
Sir Roland Ashton. By *Lady C. Long.*
Sir Wilfred's Seven Flights. By *Madame de Chatelain.*

Pilgrim's Progress. By 2 6 *Offor.*
Friend or Foe : A Tale of Sedgmoor. By the *Rev. H. C. Adams.*
Tales of Naval Adventure.
Matilda Lonsdale.
The Life of Wellington.
The Glen Luna Family.
Uncle Tom's Cabin.
Mabel Vaughan.
The Boy's Book about Indians.
Christian Melville.
The Letter of Marque.
The Swiss Family Robinson.
Evenings at Home.
Sandford and Merton.
Stepping Heavenward.
Kaloolah. By *W. S. Mayo.*
Patience Strong. By the *Author of "The Gayworthys."*
Gulliver's Travels. With Coloured Plates.
The Life of Nelson. By *Allen.*
The Young Gold Digger. By *Gerstaecker.*
Robinson Crusoe.

HALF-CROWN JUVENILES, *continued.*

s. d.

2 6 EllenMontgomery's Book-- shelf. With Coloured Illus- trations.

The Two School Girls. With Coloured Illustrations.

Melbourne House. By *Miss Wetherell.*

The Medwins of Wyke- ham. By the *Author of "Marian."*

The Young Artists.

The Boy Cavalier. By the *Rev. H. C. Adams.*

Lamb's Tales.

Stories of Old Daniel.

Extraordinary Men.

Life of Napoleon

Popular Astronomy.

The Orbs of Heaven.

The Gayworthys. By the *Author of " Faith Gartney."*

Andersen's Fairy Tales.

The Arabian Nights.

Grimm's Home Stories.

The Arctic Regions. By *P. L. Simmonds.*

Stepping Heavenward, and Aunt Jane's Hero.

Footprints on Life's Path- way.

Sceptres and Crowns, and the Flag of Truce.

Captain Cook's Voyages. Coloured Plates.

Don Quixote for Boys. Coloured Plates.

Adventures of Robin Hood. Coloured Plates.

ROUTLEDGE'S HALF-CROWN WIDE-WORLD SERIES.

In small post, 8vo, cloth gilt, well Illustrated.

2 6 The Wide, Wide World.

The Lamplighter.

The Old Helmet.

Queechy.

EllenMontgomery's Book- shelf.

The Two School Girls.

Melbourne House.

Glen Luna; or, Speculation.

Mabel Vaughan.

Patience Strong.

Most of the above are by Miss Wetherell.

ROUTLEDGE'S BOOKS FOR YOUNG READERS.

Illustrated by ABSOLON, GILBERT, HARRISON WEIR, &c., square royal, gilt, 2s. each.

s. d.

Amusing Tales for Young People. By *Mrs. Myrtle.*

The Broken Pitcher, and other Stories.

The Little Lychetts. By the *Author of " Olive,"* &c.

Historical Tales.

The Great Wonders of the World.

My First Picture Book, 36 pages of Coloured Plates. 16mo, cloth.

A Visit to the Zoological Gardens.

Aunt Bessie's Picture Book. With 96 Pages of Plates.

Little Lily's Picture Book. With 96 Pages of Plates.

The Story of a Nutcracker 2 0 With 234 Pictures.

Old Mother Hubbard's Picture Book. 36 pages of Coloured Plates.

Cock Robin's Picture Book, with 36 pages of Coloured Plates.

Aunt Mary's Sunday Picture Book.

Sunday Reading for Good Children.

The Punch and Judy Picture Book, with 36 pages of Coloured Plates.

Pussy's Picture Book, 36 pages of ditto.

Birdie's Picture Book, with 36 pages of Coloured Plates.

TWO-SHILLING GIFT-BOOKS.

With Illustrations, strongly bound in cloth.

Juvenile Tales for all Seasons.

Evenings at Donaldson Manor.

Grace and Isabel. By *M'Intosh.*

Gertrude and Eulalie.

Robert and Harold.

Robinson the Younger.

Amy Carlton.

Robinson Crusoe.

Laura Temple.

Harry and his Homes.

Our Native Land.

The Solitary Hunter.

Bundle of Sticks.

Hester and I; or, Beware of Worldliness. By *Mrs. Manners.*

The Cherry Stones. By 2 0 *Rev. H. C. Adams.*

The First of June. By *Rev. H. C. Adams.*

Rosa: A Story for Girls.

May Dundas; or, The Force of Example. By *Mrs. Geldart.*

Glimpses of Our Island Home. By *Mrs. Geldart.*

The Indian Boy. By *Rev. H. C. Adams.*

Ernie Elton at Home.

The Standard Poetry Book for Schools.

Try and Trust. By *Author of " Arthur Morland."*

Swiss Family Robinson.

Evenings at Home.

TWO-SHILLING GIFT-BOOKS, *continued*.

s. d.

2 0 Ernie Elton at School.
John Hartley.
Jack of all Trades. By *Miller.*
The Wonder Book.
Tanglewood Tales.
Archie Blake.
Inez and Emmeline.
The Orphan of Waterloo.
Maum Guinea.
Todd's Lectures to Children.
Marooner's Island.
The Mayflower. By *Mrs. Stowe.*
Anecdotes of Dogs.
Mr. Rutherford's Children.
The Play-Day Book. By *Fanny Fern.* Coloured Plates.
Emma. By *Jane Austen.*
Mansfield Park. By *Jane Austen.*
Northanger Abbey. By *Jane Austen.*
Village Sketches. By the *Rev. C.T. Whitehead.*
Spider Spinnings.
Stories for Sundays. By the *Rev. H. C. Adams.* 1st Series.
———————— 2nd Series.

Adventures among the Indians.
Cousin Aleck.
The Doctor's Birthday. By *the Rev. H. C. Adams.*
Walter's Friend. By the *Rev. H. C. Adams.*
Sweet Violets. By the *Author of "A Trap to Catch a Sunbeam."*
Ragged Robin, and other Tales. By the *Author of "A Trap to Catch a Sunbeam."*
The School Friends. By *W. H. G. Kingston.*
Sunday Evenings at Home. By the *Rev. H. C. Adams.* 1st series.
———————— 2nd series.
Wild Rose. By the *Author of "A Trap to Catch a Sunbeam."*
Snowdrop. By the *Author of "A Trap to Catch a Sunbeam.*
The Ocean Child. By *Mrs. Myrtle.*
Gulliver's Travels, with Coloured Plates.
The Lost Rifle. By the *Rev. H. C. Adams.*
Watts' Divine and Moral Songs. 60 Cuts.
Captain Cook's Voyages. With Coloured Frontispiece.

ROUTLEDGE'S EIGHTEENPENNY JUVENILES.

In square 16mo, cloth, with Illustrations by GILBERT, ABSOLON, &c.

1 6 Peasant and Prince. By *Harriet Martineau.*
Crofton Boys. By *ditto.*
Feats on the Fiord. By *do.*
Settlers at Home. By *ditto.*
Holiday Rambles ; or, The School Vacation.

Emilie the Peacemaker. By *Mrs. Geldart.*
Truth is Everything. By *Mrs. Geldart.*
Rainbows in Springtide.
Christmas Holidays. By *Miss Jane Strickland.*

EIGHTEENPENNY JUVENILES, *continued*.

s. d.
1 6

Little Drummer : A Tale of the Russian War.

Frank. By *Maria Edgeworth*.

Rosamond. By *Maria Edgeworth*.

Harry and Lucy, Little Dog Trusty, The Cherry Orchard, &c.

A Hero ; or, Philip's Book. By the *Author of " John Halifax."*

Story of an Apple. By *Lady Campbell*.

The Cabin by the Wayside.

Memoirs of a Doll. By *Mrs. Bisset*.

Black Princess.

Laura and Ellen ; or, Time Works Wonders.

Emigrant's Lost Son. By *G. H. Hall*.

Runaways (The) and the Gipsies.

Daddy Dacre's School. By *Mrs. Hall*.

British Wolf Hunters. By *Thomas Miller*.

Bow of Faith (The) ; or, Old Testament Lessons. By *Maria Wright*.

Anchor of Hope ; or, New Testament Lessons. By *Maria Wright*.

Mrs. Loudon's Young Naturalist.

Think Before you Act. Stories for Heedless Children.

Annie Maitland ; or, The Lesson of Life. By *D. Richmond*.

Lucy Elton ; or, Home and School. By the *Author of " The Twins."*

Daily Thoughts for Children. By *Mrs. Geldart*.

Holidays at Limewood.

Rose and Kate ; or, The Little Howards.

Aunt Emma. By the *Author of " Rose and Kate."*

The Island of the Rainbow. By *Mr. Newton Crossland*.

Max Frere ; or, Return Good for Evil.

The Child's First Book of Natural History. By *A. L. Bond*.

Florence the Orphan.

The Castle and Cottage. By *Perring*.

Fabulous Histories. By *Mrs. Trimmer*.

Mrs. Barbauld's Lessons.

Traditions of Palestine. By *Martineau*.

On the Sea. By *Miss Campbell*.

Games and Sports.

The Young Angler.

Athletic Sports.

Games of Skill.

Scientific Amusements.

Miriam and Rosette.

The Picture Book of Animals and Birds.

Boy Life on the Water.

Original Poems. Complete. By *A. and J. Taylor*.

Home and Foreign Birds. 150 Plates.

Wild and Domestic Animals. 150 Plates.

How Paul Arnold Made His Fortune.

The Billow and the Rock. By *Miss Martineau*.

A Year at School. By *Tom Brown*.

Æsop's Fables. With 50 Plates.

Honour and Glory.

THE SHILLING ONE-SYLLABLE SERIES.

s. d.   Square 16mo, cloth.

1 0 The Book of One Syllable. | The Sunday Book of
      Coloured Plates. | One Syllable.
    The New Book of One | Susy's Teachers. By the
      Syllable. Coloured Plates. | *Author of " Stepping Heaven-*
    Little Helps for Little | *ward."*
      Readers. Coloured Plates. | Susy's Servants. By *ditto*.

Price 1s. each.

Youens' Ball-Room Guide. With Rules and Music.
Cloth, gilt edges.

The Nursery Library. 12 Books in a Packet.

Routledge's British Reading-Book. Plate on every
page, demy 8vo, cloth.

Routledge's British Spelling-Book. Demy 8vo,
cloth. 300 Plates.

Routledge's Comic Reciter. Fcap. 8vo, boards.

———— **Popular Reciter.** Fcap. 8vo, boards.

Temperance Reciter.

Ready-Made Speeches. Fcap. 8vo, boards.

The Illustrated Language of Flowers. By Mrs.
BURKE.

THE MASTER JACK SERIES.

In small 4to, cloth, each with 48 pages of Plates, 1s. each.

1 0 Master Jack. | Nursery Rhymes.
    Mamma's Return. | The Tiger Lily.
    Nellie and Bertha. | The Lent Jewels.
    The Cousins. | Bible Stories.
    Dame Mitchell and her | My Best Frock.
      Cat. | Prince Hempseed.

With Coloured Plates, fancy boards.

1 0 My A B C Book. | The Farmyard A B C.
    Nursery Rhymes and | The Child's Book of Trades.
      Songs. | Animals and Birds.
    Old Testament A B C. | The Three Envious Men.
    Little Stories for Good | The Two Neighbours.
      Children. | For Want of a Nail.
    The History of Moses. | The Canary Bird.
    ———— Joseph.

ROUTLEDGE'S ONE-SHILLING JUVENILES.

18mo, price 1s., well printed, with Illustrations.

s. d.

Grace Greenwood's Stories for her Nephews and Nieces.

Helen's Fault. By the *Author of "Adelaide Lindsay."*

The Cousins. By *Miss M'Intosh.*

Ben Howard; or, Truth and Honesty. By *C. Adams.*

Bessie and Tom : A Book for Boys and Girls.

Beechnut : A Franconian Story. By *Jacob Abbott.*

Wallace : A Franconian Story. By *Jacob Abbott.*

Madeline. By *Jacob Abbott.*

Mary Erskine. By *Jacob Abbott.*

Mary Bell. By *Jacob Abbott.*

Visit to my Birth-place. By *Miss Bunbury.*

Carl Krinken; or, The Christmas Stocking. By *Miss Wetherell.*

Mr. Rutherford's Children. By *Miss Wetherell.*

Mr. Rutherford's Children. 2ndseries. By *Miss Wetherell.*

Emily Herbert. By *Miss M'Intosh.*

Rose and Lillie Stanhope. By *Miss M'Intosh.*

Casper. By *Miss Wetherell.*

The Brave Boy; or, Christian Heroism.

Magdalene and Raphael.

The Story of a Mouse. By *Mrs. Perring.*

Our Charlie. By *Mrs. Stowe.*

Uncle Frank's Home Stories.

Village School-feast. By 1 0 *Mrs. Perring.*

Nelly, the Gipsy Girl.

The Birthday Visit. By *Miss Wetherell*

Stories for Week Days and Sundays.

Maggie and Emma. By *Miss M'Intosh.*

Charlie and Georgie; or, The Children at Gibraltar.

Story of a Penny. By *Mrs. Perring.*

Aunt Maddy's Diamonds. By *Harriet Myrtle.*

Two School Girls. By *Miss Wetherell.*

The Widow and her Daughter. By *Miss Wetherell.*

Gertrude and her Bible. By *Miss Wetherell.*

The Rose in the Desert. By *Miss Wetherell.*

The Little Black Hen. By *Miss Wetherell.*

Martha and Rachael. By *Miss Wetherell.*

The Carpenter's Daughter. By *Miss Wetherell.*

The Story of a Cat. By *Mrs. Perring.*

Easy Poetry for Children With a Coloured Frontispiece and Vignette.

The Basket of Flowers. With a Coloured Frontispiece and Vignette.

The Story of a Dog. By *Mrs. Perring.*

Ashgrove Farm. By *Mrs. Myrtle.*

Aunt Margaret's Visit.

ONE-SHILLING JUVENILES, *continued.*

s. d.

1 0 The Angel of the Iceberg. By the *Rev. John Todd.*
Todd's Lectures for Children. 1st series.
———————— 2nd series.
Little Poems for Little Readers.
Minnie's Legacy.
Kitty's Victory.
Elise and her Rabbits.
Happy Charlie.
Annie Price.
The Little Oxleys. By *Mrs. W. Denzey Burton.*
Uncle Tom's Cabin, for Children.
Keeper's Travels in Search of His Master.
Richmond's Annals of the Poor.
Child's Illustrated Poetry Book.
Blanche and Agnes.
The Lost Chamois Hunter.
The Gates Ajar.
Mrs. Sedgwick's Pleasant Tales.

Our Poor Neighbours.
Tales in Short Words.
Watts' Songs.
Æsop's Fables.
Language and Poetry of Flowers.
Stuyvesant.
Susan Gray.
Rhymes for the Nursery. By *Anne and Jane Taylor.*
The Babes in the Basket.
The Three Sisters. By *Mrs. Perring.*
Marian Ellis. By *Mrs. Windle.*
A Kiss for a Blow.
Robert Dawson.
The Sacred Harp: A Book of Sunday Poetry.
Original Poems. (Complete Edition.)
Lily's Home. By *Mrs. Sale Barker.* 120 Illustrations.
Ellen and Frank. By *Mrs. Perring.*
Aunt Effie's Rhymes. With many new Poems.

CHRISTMAS BOOKS.

Fcap. 8vo, boards, 1s. each, with fancy covers.

1 0 Riddles and Jokes.
The Dream Book and Fortune Teller.
Acting Proverbs for the Drawing Room.
Fly Notes on Conjuring.
A Shilling's-worth of Fun.
Sensational Dramas. By *W. R. Snow.*
Family Theatricals.

Acting Charades. By *Anne Bowman.*
Pippins and Pies. By *Stirling Coyne.*
Shilling Manual of Modern Etiquette.
Plays for Children. By *Miss Walker.*
Christmas Hamper. By *Mark Lemon.*

THE HANS ANDERSEN LIBRARY.

Fcap. 8vo, gilt, 1s. each.

s. d.

The Red Shoes.
The Silver Shilling.
The Little Match-Girl.
The Darning Needle.
The Tinder Box.
The Goloshes of Fortune.
The Marsh King's
   Daughter.
The Wild Swans.
Everything in its Right
   Place.

Under the Willow Tree. _ 1 0
The Old Church Bell.
The Ice Maiden.
The Will o' the Wisp.
Poultry Meg's Family.
Put off is Not Done with.
The Snow Man.
In Sweden.
The Snow Queen.
Hardy Tin Soldier.

Each Volume contains a variety of Tales, a Frontispiece in colours, and an average of 16 other Pictures, engraved by the Brothers DALZIEL.

ROUTLEDGE'S NINEPENNY JUVENILES.

With Coloured Plates, 18mo, cloth, gilt.

Ally and her Schoolfellow.
Loyal Charlie Bentham.
Simple Stories for Children
A Child's First Book.
Story of Henrietta.
Stories from English
   History.
Life of Robinson Crusoe.
Little Paul and the Moss
   Wreaths.   [Songs.
Watts' Divine and Moral
Cobwebs to Catch Flies.

Barbauld's Hymns in Prose. 0 9
Prince Arthur.
A Winter's Wreath.
Twelve Links.
Easy Talks.
Susan and the Doll.
Juvenile Tales.
Six Short Stories.
The Captive Skylark.
Taylor's Original Poems.
    1st Series.
——— 2nd Series.

ROUTLEDGE'S MINIATURE LIBRARY.

In 64mo, 6d. each, cloth gilt, with Coloured Frontispiece.

Language of Flowers.
Etiquette for Gentlemen.
Etiquette of Courtship and
   Matrimony.
Etiquette for Ladies.

Ball Room Manual.   0 6
Handbook of Carving.
Toasts and Sentiments.
How to Dress well.

ROUTLEDGE'S SIXPENNY STORY BOOKS.

Royal 32mo, with Illustrations.
s. d.   These are also kept in Paper Covers, price 4*d.* each.

0 6 History of My Pets.
Hubert Lee.
Ellen Leslie.
Jessie Graham.
Florence Arnott.
Blind Alice.
Grace and Clara.   [hood.
Recollections of My Child-
Lazy Lawrence, and the
   White Pigeon.
The Barring Out.
The Orphans and Old Poz.
The Mimic.
The Purple Jar, and
   other Tales.
The Birthday Present,
   and the Basket Woman.
Simple Susan.
The Little Merchants.
Tale of the Universe.
Kate Campbell.
Basket of Flowers.
Babes in the Basket.
The Jewish Twins.
Children on the Plains.
Little Henry and his
   Bearer.
Learning better than
   Houses and Lands.
Maud's First Visit to her
   Aunt.
Easy Poems. Plain edges.
The Boy Captive. By
   Peter Parley.
Stories of Child Life.
The Dairyman's Daughter
Arthur's Tales for the
   Young.
Hawthorne's Gentle Boy.
Pleasant and Profitable.
Parley's Poetry and Prose.
Book about Boys. [Boys.
Arthur's Stories for Little

Egerton Roscoe.
Flora Mortimer.
Charles Hamilton.
Story of a Drop of Water.
The False Key.
The Bracelets.
Waste Not, Want Not.
Tarlton; or, Forgive and
   Forget.
The Young Cottager.
Parley's Thomas Titmouse.
Arthur's Christmas Story.
The Lost Lamb.
Arthur's Organ Boy.
Margaret Jones.
The Two School Girls.
Widow and her Daughter.
The Rose in the Desert.
The Little Black Hen.
Martha and Rachel.
The Carpenter's Daughter.
The Prince in Disguise.
Gertrude and her Bible.
The Contrast. By *Miss
   Edgeworth.*
The Grateful Negro. By
   Miss Edgeworth.
Jane Hudson.
Lina and her Cousins.
Bright-Eyed Bessie.
The Last Penny.
A Kiss for a Blow.
The Gates Ajar. Plain edges
Sunday School Reader.
Robert Dawson.
Hearty Staves. [Wealth.
Contentment better than
Robinson Crusoe.
Patient Working no Loss.
No such Word as Fail.
Edward Howard. [Girls.
Arthur's Stories for Little

ROUTLEDGE'S THREEPENNY JUVENILES.

Fcap. 8vo, with Coloured Plates, 3d.; or bound in cloth, 6d.

Sweet Violets.
White Daisy.
Only a Primrose.
Forget Me Not.
The School Friends.
The Brothers.
Alone on an Island.
The Ivory Traders.
Columbine.
Old Speedwell.
The Deadly Nightshade.
The Iris.
May.
Ragged Robin.
Jessie and Hessie.
An Artist's Holiday.
Treasure Trove.
Poor Pearl.
Nelly.
Naomi.
The White Rosebud.
Turn of the Tide.
Jolly Miller.

Raynham's Curse.　　　　o 3
Bye and Bye.
Thorns and Roses.
Wild Rose and Poppies.
Tulip and Holly.
Orange Blossoms and Eglantine.
Heart'sease and Lily of the Valley.
Snowdrop, and other Tales.
Broom, and other Tales.
Blue Bell, and other Tales.
Traveller's Joy, and other Tales.
Sunday Evenings at Home. 1st Evening.
———— 2nd Evening.
———— 3rd Evening.
———— 4th Evening.
———— 5th Evening.
———— 6th Evening.
———— 7th Evening.
———— 8th Evening.
———— 9th Evening.
———— 10th Evening.

ROUTLEDGE'S FOURPENNY JUVENILES.

For List, see Sixpenny Juveniles, on page 26.

LITTLE LADDERS TO LEARNING.

Each Illustrated with 125 Woodcuts by JOHN GILBERT, HARRISON WEIR, and others. Crown 8vo, sewed, in fancy covers, 6d. each.

Things In-doors.
What we Eat and Drink.
Animals and their Uses.
Birds and Birds' Nests.
Fishes, Butterflies, and Frogs.
Trees, Shrubs, and Flowers.

City Scenes.　　　　o 6
Rural Scenes.
Country Employments.
How Things are made.
Soldiers and Sailors.
Science and Art.
Geography and Costume.

Routledge's Nursery Literature.

ROUTLEDGE'S PENNY TOY BOOKS.

Each with Eight Coloured Plates by KRONHEIM, in Packets only,
containing the 12 sorts, 1s.

s. d.

1 0   A, Apple Pie.
The Three Bears.
Nursery Songs.
My Mother.
This Little Pig.
Farmyard A B C.
Red Riding Hood.

Jack the Giant Killer.
The Cats' Tea Party.
The Dogs' Dinner Party.
Nursery Rhymes.
Robin Redbreast.

The following vols. are formed from the above :—

1 0 **A, Apple Pie, and other Nursery Tales.** With 48
Pictures, boards.

1 6 ——————————————————— Cloth.

1 0 **The Robin Redbreast Picture Book.** Boards.

1 6 ——————————————————— Cloth.

2 0 **Jack the Giant Killer Picture Book.** With 96 Pictures, boards.

2 6 ——————————————————— Cloth.

TWOPENNY TOY BOOKS.

With Coloured Pictures by LEIGHTON Brothers, in covers, per doz. 2s.

0 2   My Mother.
Nursery Rhymes.
Our Pets.
Baby.
Mother Hubbard.

Jack the Giant Killer.
Railway A B C.
Punch and Judy.
Red Riding Hood.

Also, in One Vol.

1 6 **The Punch and Judy Picture Book.** With 36
Coloured Plates, cloth boards, 2s.

ROUTLEDGE'S THREEPENNY TOY-BOOKS.

In fancy covers, with Pictures printed in Colours;
or printed on Linen, 6d.

s. d.

Cinderella.
My First Alphabet.
Old Mother Goose.
Babes in the Wood.
This Little Pig went to Market.
The Old Woman who Lived in a Shoe.
Little Bo-peep.
Nursery Rhymes.
Farmyard Alphabet.
Jack and the Beanstalk.
John Gilpin.
Old Mother Hubbard.
Three Bears.
The House that Jack Built.

The Dogs' Dinner Party. 0 3
My Mother.
The Cats' Tea Party.
More Nursery Rhymes.
Robin Redbreast.
A, Apple Pie.
Railroad A B C.
Nursery Songs.
Nursery Ditties.
Punch and Judy.
Our Pets.
Puss in Boots.
Little Red Riding Hood.
Wild Animals.
Tame Animals.
Birds.

ROUTLEDGE'S SIXPENNY TOY-BOOKS.

Beautifully printed in Colours by Messrs. LEIGHTON Brothers,
VINCENT BROOKS, DALZIEL Brothers, and EDMUND
EVANS. In super-royal 8vo, Fancy Wrappers.

Bible Alphabet.
Nursery Alphabet.
Little Totty.
Puck and Pea-Blossom.
Old Woman and her Pig.
A, Apple Pie.
Tom Thumb's Alphabet.
Picture Alphabet.
Arthur's Alphabet.
Railroad Alphabet.
Alphabet for Good Boys and Girls.
The Seaside Alphabet.

The Enraged Miller. 0 6
The Hunchback.
How Jessie was Lost.
Grammar in Rhyme.
* Baby's Birthday.
* Pictures from the Streets.
* Lost on the Sea-Shore.
* Animals and Birds.
A Child's Fancy Dress Ball.
A Child's Evening Party.
Annie and Jack in London.
One, Two, Buckle my Shoe.

SIXPENNY TOY-BOOKS—*continued.*

s. d.

* Greedy Jem and his Little Brothers.
The Farm Yard Alphabet.
Hop o' my Thumb.
Beauty and the Beast.
Mother Hubbard.
* Happy Days of Childhood.
Little Dog Trusty.
The Cats' Tea Party.
Wild Animals.
British Animals.
* The Frog who would a-Wooing Go.
* The Faithless Parrot.
* The Farm Yard.
Horses.
Old Dame Trot.
Sing a Song of Sixpence.
The Waddling Frog.
The Old Courtier.
Multiplication Table.
Chattering Jack.
King Cole.
Prince Long Nose.

* Mary's New Doll.
* When the Cat's Away.
* Naughty Puppy.
* Children's Favourites.
Little Minnie's Child Life.
King Nutcracker.
King Grisly Beard.
Rumpelstiltskin.
The Fairy Ship.
Adventures of Puffy.
This Little Pig went to Market.
King Luckieboy's Party.
Aladdin.
Noah's Ark Alphabet.
Domestic Pets.
Nursery Rhymes.
My Mother.
The Forty Thieves.
The Three Bears.
Cinderella.
Valentine and Orson.
Puss in Boots.
Old Mother Hubbard.
The Absurd A B C.

All the above can be had Mounted on Linen, price 1s., except those marked *.

ROUTLEDGE'S NEW SERIES OF SHILLING TOY-BOOKS.

With large Original Illustrations by H. S. MARKS, J. D. WATSON, HARRISON WEIR, and KEYL, beautifully printed in Colours. Demy 4to, in stiff wrapper; or Mounted on Linen, 2s.

1 0 Nursery Rhymes.
Alphabet of Trades.
* Cinderella.
Old Testament Alphabet.
The Three Little Kittens.
The History of Five Little Pigs.
Tom Thumb's Alphabet.
Nursery Songs.

The Cats' Tea Party.
Baby.
Henny-Penny.
Peacock at Home.
Sleeping Beauty.
The Toy Primer
The Pet Lamb.
The Fair One with the Golden Locks.

SHILLING TOY-BOOKS—*continued*.

s. d.

New Testament Alphabet.
Our Farm Yard Alphabet.
The History of Moses.
The History of Joseph.
The Alphabet of Flowers.
The Life of Our Lord.
The Three Bears.
Little Red Riding Hood.
* New Tale of a Tub.
Nursery Tales.
Old Mother Hubbard.
Pictures from English History. 1st Period.
    Ditto.   2nd Period.
    Ditto.   3rd Period.
    Ditto.   4th Period.
Puss in Boots.
Tom Thumb.
Babes in the Wood.
Jack and the Beanstalk.
The Laughable A B C.
My Mother.
The Dogs' Dinner Party.
Little Dog Trusty.
The White Cat.
Dash and the Ducklings.
Reynard the Fox.
Alphabet of Fairy Tales.
Tittums and Fido.
Anne and her Mamma.

Jack the Giant Killer.   I O
Robinson Crusoe.
Cock Sparrow.
Queer Characters.
Æsop's Fables.
The Robin's Christmas Song.
The Lion's Reception.
The Frog Prince.
Goody Two Shoes.
Beauty and the Beast.
The A B C of Old Friends.
Ginger-bread.
Old Nursery Rhymes with Tunes.
The Yellow Dwarf.
Aladdin.

WILD ANIMALS.

* Lion, Elephant, Tiger.
* Leopard, Bison, Wolf.
* Bear, Hyæna, Zebra.
* Hippopotamus, Rhinoceros, Giraffe.

TAME ANIMALS.

* Horse, Cow, Sheep.
* Donkey, Pet Dog, Goat.
* Rabbit, Guinea Pig, Dog.
* Pig, Pony, Cat.

All the above can be had Mounted on Linen, 2s., except those marked*.

Lightning Source UK Ltd.
Milton Keynes UK
UKHW020656110721
386991UK00003B/28